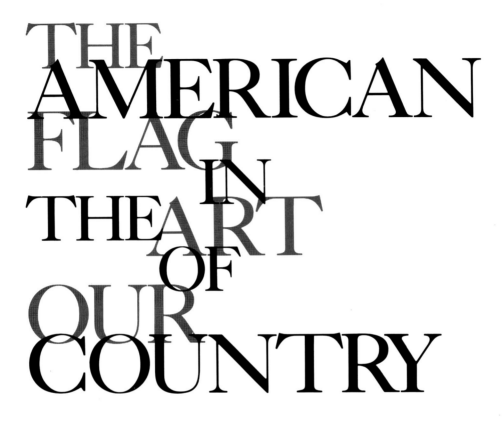

THE AMERICAN FLAG IN THE ART OF OUR COUNTRY

JUNE 14 THROUGH NOVEMBER 14, 1976

ALLENTOWN ART MUSEUM

2

FOREWORD

The bicentennial year has been a bonus for the study of American art history, because in addition to many publications, museums throughout the nation have staged several important exhibitions. As a tribute to our first two hundred years, these exhibitions feature either major movements by well-known artists or new works created by those who are looking into the future. It is a very exciting and fitting way to celebrate the Bicentennial.

Research on the Allentown Art Museum's current offering, THE AMERICAN FLAG IN THE ART OF OUR COUNTRY, began in 1972. Since then, colleagues and friends have thoughtfully suggested candidates to be included in the show. Many ideas were accepted or investigated until now we have close to 150 paintings, sculpture, drawings and prints, plus some decorative and "popular" art objects. The works, which date from 1786 to 1976, project a survey of American art using the flag as chief or contributing subject matter.

Of course, an exhibition of this stature would be impossible without generous lenders and donors. The Museum is indebted to 30 public institutions, 17 private collectors, 14 art dealers and 13 individual artists who permitted us to borrow their holdings for almost a six-month period. Further indispensable sponsorship is equally divided between grants from the National Endowment for the Arts (a Federal agency), the Lehigh County Bicentennial Commission, and Mack Trucks, Inc., whose corporate headquarters are in Allentown. Sincere gratitude goes to all.

Initial encouragement to work on the project came from the Museum's Board of Trustees, headed by President Bernard Berman. The task of seeing the job to completion was in the capable hands of Mrs. Virginia Lisk and Mrs. Dolores O'Mara. It was they who typed letters of inquiry and thanks; investigated procedures of insurance and shipping; saw after details of the catalogue and promotion, plus much, much more. They have my personal appreciation.

Thanks also goes to the Museum's comptroller, Mrs. Barbara Strohl, who applied for needed grants and kept their careful accounting; to Ms. Ann Bressoud who, during the summer of 1975, composed most of the docent biographical notes; and to David Miller, building superintendent, who has so capably installed one of the largest temporary displays in the Museum's history.

Finally, thanks are given to Mrs. Marie-Louise Mastai who wrote the article on historic flags as art and to her husband Boleslaw whom she joined in offering information and enthusiasm. Praise also is extended to Owen Scott who designed this catalogue.

Speaking for lenders of art, the sponsors, Museum members, trustees, staff and others who helped make this exhibition possible, I offer this exhibition for the continued celebration of our Bicentennial and for the enjoyment of all who visit the Lehigh Valley in 1976.

Richard N. Gregg

INTRODUCTION

Symbols have always been a basic tool of civilization. But these are not hidden messages. Rather, they are language which is more generally understood than words: they are based upon the times and places where they were used; the importance of the subject to daily life; and individual perceptive, or learned knowledge. In effect, symbols are a shorthand method of interpreting a complicated story.

A familiar symbol in the form of a street sign alerts motorists to crossing students; a skull and crossbones on a medicine bottle represents death; a white Easter lily suggests virgin purity; and the United States flag stands for the glory of our country.

In the past 200 years nationalistic symbolism in American arts and crafts has included bald-headed eagles, Uncle Sam, likenesses of Washington or Lincoln, doves of peace or the Liberty Bell. But none of these dominate as much as the Stars and Stripes. Few international flags have inspired such artistic veneration.

The old Red, White and Blue has been used repeatedly in the visual arts to symbolize loyalty, sacrifice, heroism and other important patriotic sentiments. This has been true not only of the early years but through the 19th and early 20th centuries as well.

Contemporary work sometimes emphasizes the flag only as design and color. On other occasions it expresses discontent and sarcasm. Examples of these approaches are included with the more patriotic works to reflect living artists' sincere feelings and beliefs.

This is a subjective exhibition and microscopic in terms of the total use of the American flag in the art of our country. There are hundreds more paintings and objects which could have successfully enlarged the topic — if they had been available and if we had found the means.

But rather than a comprehensive history, our purpose is to hint at the rich variety of art in our land using an important single "motif." Thus, although there are many profound works, there also are a few of high humor and spirit.

A symbol is only meaningful if kept alive and valid. It is assumed this pertains to our colorful sovereign emblem so imaginatively portrayed here by some of America's most creative minds.
R.N.G.

THE AMERICAN FLAG AS A FORM OF ART IN OUR COUNTRY

The theme of the Stars and Stripes always has been significant *in* the art of our country. We may be surprised to learn that quite independently flags have also existed *as* art. From its origin through the mid-19th century, many imaginative Americans enjoyed creating versions of the beloved emblem; indeed, flag designs are an important part of the whole gamut of our country's folk art heritage.

By the second decade of the 19th century, strict flag regulations were issued that effectively put an end to this creativity. In fact, these rules were obeyed so conscientiously that even the memory of previous flag designs was erased. Moreover, standard flag books recognized only the so-called "official" flags. Representation of flags was usually of military examples only and even these were merely diagrams showing the increase in the number of stars as new states joined the union.

As a result, the American public nearly lost all knowledge of a fascinating part of its heritage, the brilliantly imaginative civilian flags, "the flags of the free."

"Free" is the key word to understanding the development of the flag as we know it today, for it was only in America that such latitude was enjoyed in the interpretation of the national emblem. In other lands, precise regulations had been set down in ancient times, and these were strictly enforced. On the contrary, our Flag Resolution of June 14, 1777, gave only the most general of directives: ". . . 13 stripes alternate red and white . . . 13 stars white in a blue field . . ." At the start, even these instructions were not always adhered to, often because polished American gentlemen of that age were still keenly conscious of heraldic regulations. According to these the proper order of the stripes should have been "white and red," and the stars must have six rays or more (a five-pointed shape representing *not* a star, but the rowel on a knight's spur).

Nevertheless, the symbols as we now know them soon gained wide acceptance. The number of the stripes was permanently set to thirteen and from then on, it was on the arrangement of the stars in the left-hand corner that designers bestowed apparently inexhaustible ingenuity. The exuberance and versatility of the interpretations brought forth during the 130-odd years when there were no curbs on designing American flags is demonstrated in representative panoply depicted in "Two Centuries of the Stars and Stripes" (last illustration in this catalogue). The examples shown there are not, as viewers might think, imaginary; they are absolutely faithful miniature portrayals of actual flags — antique originals, each one-of-a-kind. As they have been grouped chronologically, they present a thumbnail sketch of stars and stripes development.

The first tier from the bottom covers the period from the War of Independence to the eve of the Civil War and shows a number of the early patterns: quincuncial, wreath, diamond, great star, etc. The first flag in that group is "The Prisoner's Flag" — also seen here in the exhibition as an actual size trompe l'oeil rendering made in England by an American prisoner of war who placed the stars in a quincuncial pattern that, with the proper multiplication, is also the pattern chosen for the present flag of fifty stars.

In the central tier, the range is from the outbreak of the Civil War through the era of the First Centennial, and the stylistic evolution is from strikingly original conceptions ("Snowflakes Flag," "Great Flower Flag," "Great Medallion," "Hour-glass," and "Global" flags) to arrangements based on a square or rectangular composition of rows of stars (the "phalanx" or battalion pattern) that gained favor during the Civil War, and which became firmly established as the one acceptable pattern in modern times.

The examples in the highest tier represent the last efforts at unorthodox flag designing in America: the flag at left of center was designed by Wayne Whipple and deservedly came very close to being adopted as the national flag. The flag of 48 stars is seen in a light-hearted tri-color version created to celebrate the victory of the Allies in World War I. The succession of identical flags beyond this symbolizes the perfectly regular version still familiar to many, since it was used from 1912 to 1958. The flag of 49 stars had a life span of only one year, and differed only in that the stars were placed in staggered instead of regular rows.

It is fortunate indeed that these antique originals should have survived, but sad to wonder how many more must have been destroyed when they had outlived their usefulness. Happily, the record is supplemented in ship paintings and views of towns, forts, etc. — precisely of the sort shown in this exhibition.

The artists contributed far more than is often realized to the development of the design of the flag. In all likelihood, the flags they portrayed are versions now lost but once in use, and perhaps even the artist's own creation. One may reasonably look in this light at the beautiful starry wreath of heraldic multi-rayed stars by Charles Wilson Peale in his "Portrait of Washington," 1779; the flag with its stars in a "square formation" in John Trumbull's "Surrender at Saratoga;" and the tri-color striped standard in the same artist's brilliant sketch for the "Surrender at Yorktown." All were once considered pure flights of fancy, but the tri-colored standard has been fully vindicated by scholarly research.

An American artist was first to "fly" an American flag on British soil: John Singleton Copley hastened to add an American flag atop the ship he had depicted in the background of a portrait, immediately after he had heard the speech in which the king recognized American independence.

In 1851, when Rudolf Friedrich Kurz depicted on the walls of Fort Union on the Missouri River a large and beautiful "eagle flag," he was entitled to triple credit: as portrayer, as designer and as maker of the flag — which is remarkably close compositionally to the "Kingsboro Eagle Flag" shown at the center of the lowest tier in "Two Centuries of the Stars and Stripes." The Kingsboro Flag is one of the very few extant signed by their creators — in this instance, an artist who has identified himself merely as "Holmes." Evidence abounds that, to a surprisingly late date, the flag *in* the art of our country and the flag *as* art of our country were conjoined so closely as to make demarcation well nigh impossible.

Another aspect of the phenomenon holds special appeal for the modern mind. In manipulation of the two geometric elements—stars and stripes—the early designers of "Old Glory" initiated two avant-garde movements: geometric abstraction and kinetics. This came about in the rare but admirable instances when genial anonymous American artists of the past strove to portray "the stars in orbit." Their goal was to depict the "new constellation" called for by the Flag Resolution not merely in static beauty, but truly endowed with "this very quality of motion" which had been extolled by John D. Long as early as 1848 as the supreme characteristic of the stars and stripes.

M. L. D'Otrange Mastai

NOTE: *All exhibition catalogue entries are chronological, known date of the work preceding that of circa. Height in inches and centimeters comes before width. An alphabetical listing of artists represented appears on page 90. Lenders' names are on page 91.*

The Surrender of Cornwallis at Yorktown, 1787
JOHN TRUMBULL (1756-1843)
Oil on canvas, 14⁹⁄₁₆ x 21¾, 37 x 55
Lent Anonymously

View of the Cannon House and Wharf, 1792
JONATHAN BUDINGTON (active 1792-1812)
Oil on wood panel, 44 x 80, 111 x 202
Lent by H. Richard Dietrich, Jr.

The Frigate 'United States' Forty-four Guns, c. 1798
PATRICK HAYES (active late 18th century), Attributed to
Gouache on paper, 12½ x 15¼, 32 x 39
Lent by Warren Sturgis

Winter, early 19th century
WILLIAM RUSH (1756-1833), Studio of
Painted wood, 27, 68
Lent by Victor D. Spark

A Parade Passing Independence Hall, Philadelphia, c. 1812
JOHN LEWIS KRIMMEL (1789-1821)
Watercolor, ink and pencil, 7⅝ x 11¾, 18 x 30
Lent by Springfield Art Museum, Missouri

Election Day at the State House, 1816
JOHN LEWIS KRIMMEL
India ink and watercolor, 8½ x 13, 23 x 33
Lent by The Historical Society of Pennsylvania

Washington Welcomed (Philadelphia?), c. 1820
JOHN LEWIS KRIMMEL
Oil on canvas, 17½ x 22½, 44 x 58
Lent by Berry-Hill Galleries

Naval Engagement Between the Constitution and Guerrière, August 18, 1812, c. 1814
THOMAS BIRCH (1779-1851)
Oil on canvas, 29 x 36, 74 x 91
Lent by The Historical Society of Pennsylvania

Peace of Ghent 1814 and Triumph of America, 1815
ALEXIS CHATAIGNER (1772-1817) after M. Plantou (active 1815-1830)
Etching and engraving, 9¾ x 14¼, 24.5 x 36.2
Lent by The Library of Congress

Memorial to George Washington, c. 1815
ANONYMOUS
Watercolor, 15$\frac{13}{16}$ x 10$\frac{5}{16}$, 40 x 27
Lent by Philadelphia Museum of Art,
The Edgar William and Bernice Chrysler Garbisch Collection

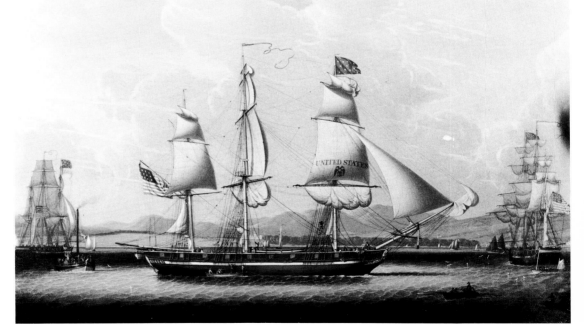

Packet Ship 'United States' 1817
ROBERT SALMON (1775-1842)
Oil on canvas, 22$\frac{1}{4}$ x 36$\frac{1}{4}$, 56 x 92
Lent by Peabody Museum

13

Battle of Monterey, the Americans Forcing Their Way to the Main Plaza,
September 23, 1846
ANONYMOUS, Lithograph by N. Currier, New York
Hand-colored lithograph, 8½ x 12¾, 21 x 32
Lent by The Library of Congress

Naval Heroes of the United States, 1846
ANONYMOUS, Lithograph by N. Currier, New York
Hand-colored lithograph, 10 x 13, 25 x 33
Lent by The Library of Congress

The Life and Age of Man, 1848
ANONYMOUS, Lithograph printed by James Baillie, New York (active 1838-1855)
Hand-colored lithograph, 8½ x 12¾, 21 x 32
Lent by The Library of Congress

Stockton, October, 1849
W.H. CREASY (19th century)
Watercolor, 17½ x 20¾, 44 x 51
Lent by Pioneer Museum and Haggin Galleries

Bunkerhill, 1838
JURGAN FREDERICK HUGE (1809-1879)
Watercolor, 19 x 32, 48 x 81
Lent by The Mariners Museum

Washington Crossing the Delaware, c. 1851-1852
EMANUEL G. LEUTZE (1816-1868), Attributed to
Oil on canvas, 27 x 40½, 69 x 103
Lent by The Los Angeles Athletic Club

Washington Crossing the Delaware, 1853
EMANUEL G. LEUTZE,
Engraved by Paul Girardet (1821-1893)
Engraving, subscription proof, 22⅜ x 38⅛, 56 x 96
Lent by Prints Division, The New York Public Library,
Astor, Lenox and Tilden Foundations

Washington Crossing the Delaware on the Evening of December 25, 1776
Previous to the Battle of Trenton, after 1855
CURRIER & IVES (19th century)
Colored lithograph, 8 x 12⅛, 20 x 30
Lent by Museum of the City of New York,
The Harry T. Peters Collection

George Washington Crossing the Delaware, c. 1860
ANONYMOUS (19th century)
Oil on canvas, 30¼ x 40¼, 77 x 102
Lent by Philadelphia Museum of Art,
The Edgar William and Bernice Chrysler Garbisch Collection

The Young America Schottisch, 1855
ANONYMOUS, Lithograph by Sarony and Co., New York
Colored lithograph, 13½ x 10, 34 x 25
Lent by The Library of Congress

Young '76, c. 1855
CHARLES G. CREHEN (1829-c. 1890)
Oil on canvas, 27¼ x 22, 69 x 56
Lent by The New York Historical Society

The Pie Man (A Civic Procession), 1856
WILLIAM E. WINNER (c. 1815-1883)
Oil on canvas, 24 x 20, 61 x 51
Lent by The Historical Society of Pennsylvania

Eagle Hotel, Caleb Yohe, Proprietor, Bethlehem, Pennsylvania, c. 1860
ANONYMOUS
Watercolor and rinceau, 17 x 21, 43 x 53
Lent by Annie S. Kemerer Museum

J. Schreiber and Company's Chewing Tobacco, c. 1860
ANONYMOUS, Lithograph by W. J. Morgan and Co., Cleveland (19th century)
Colored lithograph, 9¼ x 11¾, 23 x 30
Lent by The Library of Congress

The Glorious Fourth of July, c. 1860
ARNOUD WYDEVELD (active 1855-1862)
Oil on canvas, 30¼ x 25, 77 x 64
Lent by Kennedy Galleries, Inc.

The Golden Eagle, c. 1860
ANONYMOUS (19th century)
Embroidery, silk floss on satin, 16 x 20, 40.5 x 50.5
Lent by Mr. and Mrs. Boleslaw Mastai

Elephant On a Tightrope With Star-Spangled Banners, c. 1860
EDUARD SINGER (active 1860, German)
Hand-colored lithograph, 18 x 26, 46 x 66
Lent by Mr. and Mrs. Boleslaw Mastai

Box, second half of 19th century
ANONYMOUS (Japanese)
Lacquer on wood with silver bow, 2¼ x 3, 6 x 7.5
Lent by Mr. and Mrs. Boleslaw Mastai

Jenny Lind Mirror, second half of 19th century
ANONYMOUS
Cast iron and glass, 19 x 13, 48 x 33
Lent by Mr. and Mrs. Boleslaw Mastai

Torchlight Parade by General Blenker's Division in Honor of
General McClellan's Promotion to Commander-in-Chief of the Army,
Washington, D.C., November 3, 1861
ALFRED R. WAUD (1828-1891)
Pencil and Chinese white on tan paper, 7½ x 21½, 19 x 55
Lent by The Library of Congress

Our Heaven Born Banner, 1861
WILLIAM BAULY (mid 19th century), Lithograph printed by Sarony, Major and Knapp, New York
Colored lithograph, 8½ x 12½, 21 x 32
Lent by The Library of Congress

The American Declaration of Independence Illustrated, 1861
ANONYMOUS, Lithograph by L. Prang and Company, Boston
Colored lithograph, 18½ x 13¼, 47 x 33
Lent by The Library of Congress

For President Abram Lincoln, For Vice-President Hannibal Hamlin, 1861
ANONYMOUS
Printed cloth, 23 x 35, 59 x 89
Lent by The Library of Congress

Mr. Pennington's Steam Balloon, mid 19th century
ANONYMOUS
Colored woodcut, 12 x 18, 30 x 46
Lent by The Library of Congress

The American Flag. A New National Lyric, 1862
ANONYMOUS, Printed by Gilmour and Dean (19th century)
Colored lithograph, sheet music, 14¼ x 10¼, 36 x 26
Lent by The Library of Congress

Battle of Gettysburg, Pennsylvania, July 1-3, 1863
ALFRED R. WAUD
Pencil and Chinese white on tan paper, 13½ x 20¾, 34 x 52
Lent by The Library of Congress

Thanksgiving Day, November 26, 1853, 1863
ADDIE HARRINGTON (19th century)
Oil on canvas, 27½ x 22½, 70 x 57
Lent by Hirschl & Adler Galleries

Ball of 5th Corps, 1st Division (General Bartlett) Near Beverly Ford,
Virginia, March 16, 1864
EDWIN FORBES (1839-1895)
Pencil on paper, 6½ x 10, 16 x 25
Lent by The Library of Congress

Our Flag, 1864
FREDERICK EDWIN CHURCH (1826-1900)
Oil on canvas, 21½ x 13½, 52 x 34
Lent by Indianapolis Museum of Art

Barbara Frietsche and the American Flag, 1862-1870
ANONYMOUS (19th century)
Oil on canvas, 36½ x 28½, 92 x 72
Lent by Berry-Hill Galleries

Isham's Celebrated Stomach Bitters, 1864
ANONYMOUS, Lithograph printed by Edward Mendel, Chicago
Colored lithograph, 6 x 2¼, 15 x 6
Lent by The Library of Congress

Allegory of Freedom, c. 1863
ANONYMOUS (19th century)
Oil on canvas, 37⅛ x 43, 95 x 110
Lent by National Gallery of Art,
Gift of Edgar William and Bernice Chrysler Garbisch, 1955

Uncle Sam on a Bicycle, late 19th century
ANONYMOUS
Wood and metal, painted, 33 x 55, 84 x 139
Lent by Mr. and Mrs. Leo Rabkin

Flag Weathervane, late 19th century
ANONYMOUS (New England)
Painted sheet metal with wooden hammer, 34, 48
Lent by The Barenholtz Collection

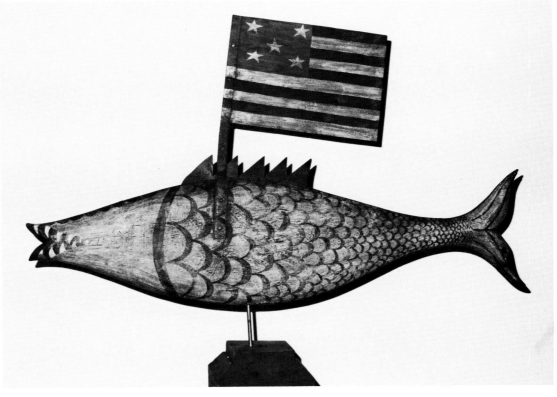

Fish Weathervane, late 19th century
ANONYMOUS
Sheet iron and wood, 26½ x 45½, 67 x 115
Lent Anonymously

Battle of Fredericksburg, c. 1862
FREDERICK F. CAVADA (1832-1871)
Oil on canvas, 24 x 36, 61 x 91
Lent by The Historical Society of Pennsylvania

Beaded Bandolier Bag, Chippewa Tribe, c. 1875
ANONYMOUS
Beads on cloth, 34½ x 14½, 87 x 37
Lent by Museum of the American Indian, Heye Foundation

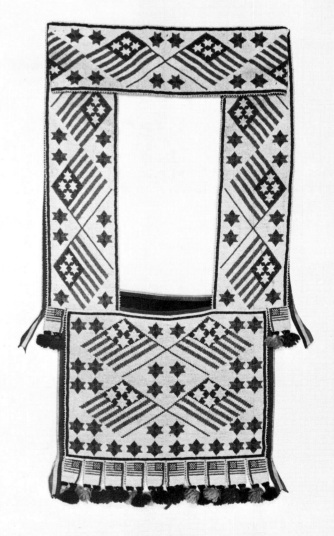

Goddess of Liberty, c. 1875
ANONYMOUS
Copper, gilt and polychrome, 34¾, 88
Lent by Mr. and Mrs. G. William Holland

Yankee Doodle 1776, 1875
ASAPH M. WILLARD, (1786-1880), Published by J. F. Ryder, Cleveland
Lithograph by Clay, Cosack and Company, Buffalo
Colored lithograph, 24 x 18, 61 x 46
Lent by The Library of Congress

The Signing of the Declaration of Independence, 1876
After the 1786 painting by John Trumbull
Colored lithograph, 22 x 28, 56 x 71
Lent by The Dinwiddie Mantle and Victorius Collection

Uncle Sam on the Range, 1876
ANONYMOUS, Lithograph by Schumacher and Ettlinger
Colored lithograph, 20 x 24, 50 x 61
Lent by The Library of Congress

Street Car Travel During the Centennial, c. 1876
EDWIN S. HALEY (late 19th century)
Oil on canvas, 42½ x 54, 108 x 137
Lent by The Historical Society of Pennsylvania

Historical Monument of the American Republic, 1873-1876
ERASTUS SALISBURY FIELD (1805-1900)
Photo-engraving, 15 x 22¾, 38 x 57
Lent by Museum of Fine Arts, Springfield, Massachusetts,
Gift of Mrs. Victor H. Wesson

Observation Balloon Experiment at the Japanese Navy Department
(Established 1872) in Chikuji, Tokyo. View from Seiyokan, c. 1880
YOSHITORA (19th century Japanese)
Color woodcut, two parts joined in center, total size 14¼ x 19, 36 x 48
Lent by The Library of Congress

Washington's Triumphal Entry into New York in 1783, c. 1880
ANONYMOUS
Oil, needlework in yarn, sequins, plastic buttons on canvas, 53 x 53, 135 x 135
Lent by Abby Aldrich Rockefeller Folk Art Collection

Captain W. F. Bartlett and Lieutenant-Colonel F. W. Palfrey at Camp Benton,
Maryland, November 1861, 1881
WINSLOW HOMER (1836-1910)
Oil on canvas, 21 x 33, 53 x 84
Lent by The Trustees of the Boston Public Library

Her Atonement. Off to the War '62, 1883
ANONYMOUS, Poster lithograph by Strobridge & Company, New York
Colored lithograph, 26 x 36, 66 x 93
Lent by The Library of Congress

The Star Spangled Banner
ANONYMOUS, Lithograph by Currier & Ives
Hand-colored lithograph, 13 x 9, 33 x 23
Lent by Prints Division, The New York Public Library,
Astor, Lenox and Tilden Foundations

Battle of Quasimas near Santiago, June 24, 1898, 1899
ANONYMOUS, Lithograph by Kurz & Allison, Chicago
Colored lithograph, 20 x 26, 51 x 66
Lent by The Library of Congress

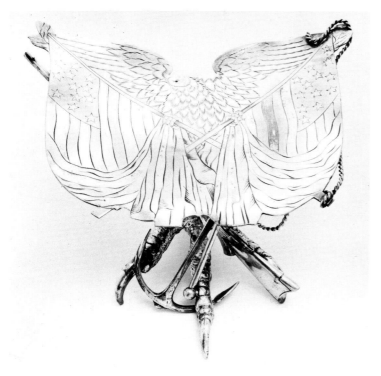

Dish, late 19th century
PAIRPONT MANUFACTURING COMPANY (New Bedford, Ma.)
Silver, 3 x 7½, 7.5 x 19
Lent by Mr. and Mrs. Boleslaw Mastai

34

Boat Landing, c. 1900
MAURICE PRENDERGAST (1859-1924)
Watercolor, 11¾ x 20¼, 30 x 51
Lent by Wadsworth Atheneum,
Gift of George A. Gay, 1941

The American Flag, c. 1900
ANONYMOUS
Embroidery on linen, 20 x 18, 50.5 x 45.5
Lent by Mr. and Mrs. Boleslaw Mastai

Landscape with Railroad Trestle, early 20th century
ANONYMOUS
Painted glass with Mother of Pearl, 14 x 30, 36 x 76
Lent by Mr. and Mrs. Leo Rabkin

Whirligig with Trailing Flag, early 20th century
ANONYMOUS
Painted wood and tin, 12 x 17½ x 13 d., 30 x 44 x 33
Lent by Mr. and Mrs. Leo Rabkin

Wind-up Toy Clown, 20th century
ANONYMOUS, Made by J. Chein and Company
Painted tin, 4¾ x 2 x 1¾ d., 12 x 5 x 2
Lent by Mr. and Mrs. Leo Rabkin

American Flag Quilt, c. 1907-1912
ANONYMOUS
Cotton, 84 x 83¾, 213 x 212
Lent by Daughters of Hawaii at Queen Emma Summer Palace

The Eagles' Flag, 1907
ANONYMOUS
Oil print on cloth, 23 x 23, 58 x 58
Lent by Mr. and Mrs. Boleslaw Mastai

Flag Painting, 1907
ANONYMOUS
Oil on canvas, 29 x 68, 73.5 x 172
Lent by Kronen Gallery

The Franco-Anglo-American Flag, early 20th century
ANONYMOUS
Oil print in color, 10 x 14, 25.2 x 35.5
Lent by Mr. and Mrs. Boleslaw Mastai

Pillow, 1911
ANONYMOUS (American Indian)
Glass beads on leather, 17 x 18, 43 x 45.5
Lent by Mr. and Mrs. Boleslaw Mastai

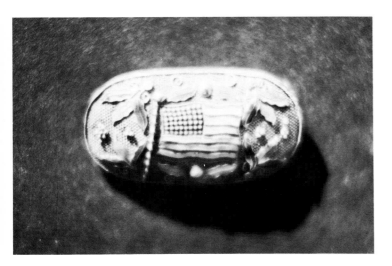

Brooch, 1912
ANONYMOUS (Chinese)
Silver filigree with enamel, 1 x 2, 2.5 x 5
Lent by Mr. and Mrs. Boleslaw Mastai

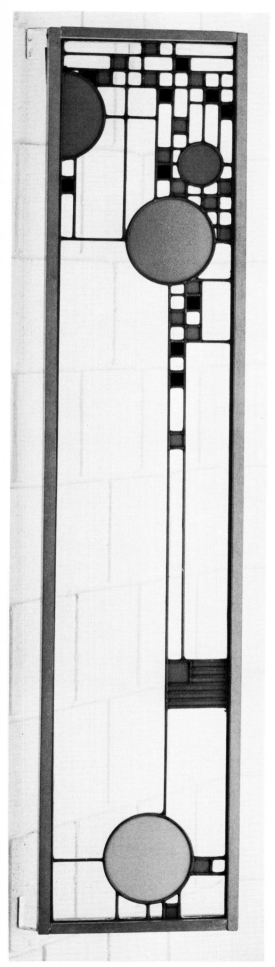

Window from the Avery Coonley Playhouse, Riverside, Illinois, 1912
FRANK LLOYD WRIGHT (1867-1959)
Leaded glass, 62 x 13⅝, 157 x 33
Lent by Mr. and Mrs. Walter A. Netsch

Fifth Avenue, April Morning, 1917
CHILDE HASSAM (1859-1935)
Watercolor, 11½ x 10¾, 29 x 27
Lent by The University of Nebraska Art Galleries, F. M. Hall Collection
(only through September 26)

Be a U.S. Marine, c. 1914-1918
JAMES MONTGOMERY FLAGG (1877-1935)
Colored lithograph, 39½ x 27½, 100 x 70
Lent by The Library of Congress

The Service Flag, 1918
CHILDE HASSAM
Lithograph, 9 x 6, 23 x 15
Lent by Prints Division, The New York Public Library,
Astor, Lenox and Tilden Foundations

Lafayette Street, New York, 1918
CHILDE HASSAM
Lithograph, 14½ x 10⅞, 37 x 27
Lent by Prints Division, The New York Public Library,
Astor, Lenox and Tilden Foundations

Allies Day, May 1917
CHILDE HASSAM
Oil on canvas, 36¾ x 30¼, 93 x 77
Lent by National Gallery of Art,
Gift of Ethelyn McKinney in Memory of Her Brother, Glenn Ford McKinney, 1943

Armistice Night, 1918
GEORGE LUKS (1867-1933)
Oil on canvas, 37 x 68¾, 94 x 175
Lent by Whitney Museum of American Art

Victory Day, May 1919, 9:30 A.M.
CHILDE HASSAM
Oil on canvas, 36 x 22, 91 x 56
Lent by The American Academy of Arts and Letters

Flags, Fifth Avenue, 1918
CHILDE HASSAM
Watercolor, $13\frac{5}{8}$ x $9\frac{3}{8}$, 33 x 23
Lent by Dallas Museum of Fine Arts,
The Munger Fund

Arlington Street Church, c. 1917
ARTHUR C. GOODWIN (1864-1929)
Oil on canvas, 25 x 30, 64 x 74
Lent by Robert C. Vose, Jr.

Rally Round the Flag, Boys!, c. 1917
ANONYMOUS
Lithograph and collage, 14 x 6, 35.5 x 15
Lent by Mr. and Mrs. Boleslaw Mastai

Armistice Day, 1918
GIFFORD R. BEAL (1879-1956)
Oil on canvas, 48 x 36, 121 x 91
Lent by Indiana University Art Museum, William Lowe Bryan Memorial Collection

Flags, 1918
THEODORE EARL BUTLER (born 1894)
Oil on canvas, 42¼ x 27¼, 112 x 69
Lent by Mr. and Mrs. Joe M. Leonard, Jr.

Flag Day, n.d.
JANE PETERSON (1876-1965)
Gouache and charcoal, 23⅛ x 17⅜, 58 x 44
Lent by Hirschl & Adler Galleries

At the Beach, c. 1918
WILLIAM GLACKENS (1870-1938)
Oil on canvas, 25 x 30, 64 x 76
Lent by The Newark Museum

Columbia, 1919
CHARLES DEMUTH (1883-1935)
Watercolor, 11$\frac{15}{16}$ x 8, 30 x 20
Lent by The Columbus Gallery of Fine Arts,
Ferdinand Howald Collection

Wild West Show, 1922
OTTO DIX (1891-1969, German)
Drypoint, painted black, 13⅝ x 12⅟₁₆, 33 x 30
Lent by The Museum of Modern Art, Gift of Victor S. Riesenfeld

Girard Trust Building, Philadelphia, c. 1922
PAULETTE VAN ROEKINS (born 1896)
Oil on board, 13¼ x 17¼, 34 x 44
Allentown Art Museum Collection,
Gift of Mr. and Mrs. J. I. Rodale, 1961

Pouch, 1925
ANONYMOUS (American Indian)
Beads, cloth, cardboard, 8 x 6¾ x 5½ deep, 20 x 17 x 14
Lent by Mr. and Mrs. Leo Rabkin

Columbia Gives to Her Son the Accolade
of the New Chivalry of Humanity, c. 1919
E. H. BLASHFIELD (1848-1936)
Hand-colored lithograph, 16 x 12, 40.5 x 30.5
Lent by Mr. and Mrs. Boleslaw Mastai

Uncle Sam, 1927
NORMAN ROCKWELL (born 1894)
Oil on canvas, 34 x 24, 86 x 62
Lent by Edna B. Wilmot

Portrait of Charles Lindbergh, 1927
PIERO TOLENTINI (first half of 20th century, Italian)
Oil on canvas, 39 x 32, 99 x 81
Lent by Mr. and Mrs. Boleslaw Mastai

54

Drooping American Flag, c. 1930
GUY PENE DU BOIS (1884-1958)
Oil on canvas, 18 x 24, 46 x 61
Lent by M. Knoedler & Company, Inc.

Harmony of the Polish and American National Anthems
ROMAN DZIKOWSKI (20th century, Polish)
Watercolor, 14 x 10, 35.5 x 25.5
Lent by Mr. and Mrs. Boleslaw Mastai

Touching Up, c. 1931-1932
JOHN KANE
Oil on canvas, 20¾ x 27, 53 x 69
Lent by Museum of Art, Carnegie Institute

Lincoln's Gettysburg Address, c. 1931-1932
JOHN KANE (1860-1934)
Oil on canvas, 25¾ x 19¼, 66 x 48
Lent by M. Knoedler & Company, Inc.

Flag Day, 1935
WILLIAM DORIANI (born 1891)
Oil on canvas, 12¼ x 38⅝, 31 x 97
Lent by The Museum of Modern Art,
The Sidney and Harriet Janis Collection, 1967

Commodore Perry and Henson at the North Pole, 1945
W. H. JOHNSON (1901-1970)
Oil on board, 27½ x 35, 70 x 89
Lent by Museum of African Art

Parade, 1947
STEVAN DOHANOS (born 1907)
Tempera, 21 x 16½, 53 x 41
Lent by the Artist

Flag Above White With Collage, 1955
JASPER JOHNS (born 1930)
Encaustic and collage on canvas, 22½ x 19¼, 57 x 50
Lent by the Artist

Flags, 1967-1968
JASPER JOHNS
Colored lithograph, $34\frac{5}{8}$ x $25\frac{7}{8}$, 87 x 65
Lent by The Museum of Modern Art,
Gift of the Celeste and Armand Bartos Foundation

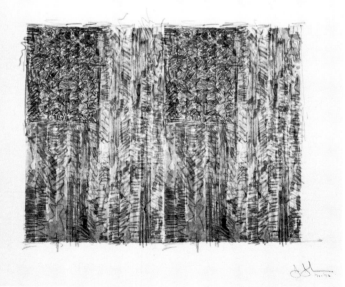

Two Flags, 1972
JASPER JOHNS
Lithograph with graphite, 22 x $27\frac{1}{2}$, 57 x 69
Lent by The Museum of Modern Art, Gift of Celeste Bartos

The Last Civil War Veteran, 1961
LARRY RIVERS (born 1923)
Oil on canvas, 82½ x 64½, 209 x 163
Lent by Martha Jackson Collection, Courtesy Walker Art Center

Last Civil War Veteran. II, 1961
LARRY RIVERS
Colored lithograph, 17½ x 14¾, 44 x 37
Lent by The Museum of Modern Art,
Gift of the Celeste and Armand Bartos Foundation

Flag I, 1973
JASPER JOHNS
Serigraph of 31 screens, 39/66, 27¼ x 35, 69 x 89
Lent by Greenville County Museum of Art

Two Flags, 1972
JASPER JOHNS
Lithograph, 24¹⁵⁄₁₆ x 20¼, 63 x 51
Lent by The Museum of Modern Art, Gift of Celeste Bartos

Dallas III — November 22, 1963, 1964
ANTONIO FRASCONI (born 1919)
Woodcut, 36 x 24, 91 x 61
Lent by Terry Dintenfass, Inc.

New Old Glory Banner, 1964
ROBERT INDIANA (born 1928)
Applique cloth, 72 x 48, 182 x 122
Lent by Mr. and Mrs. Walter A. Netsch

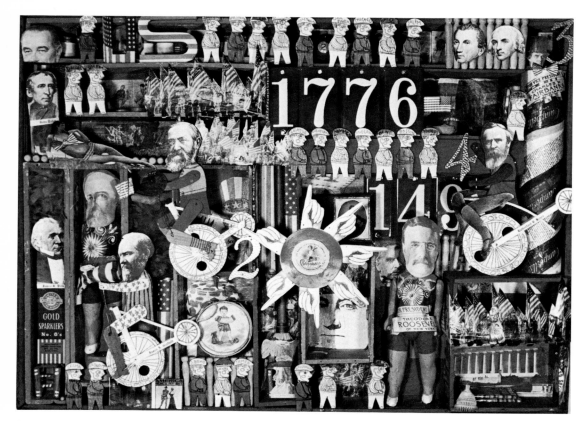

Assemblage, 1776, 1965
CYRIL MILES
Mixed media, 30 x 40½ x 7 d., 76 x 102 x 18
Lent by the Artist

We Shall Overcome: Santos, U.S.A., 1965
CYRIL MILES (born 1918)
Watercolor and collage on canvas, 94 x 70, 258 x 177
Lent by the Artist

Explorers' Dinner, 1967
BYRON BURFORD (born 1920)
Lithograph, 25¾ x 30½, 65 x 77
Lent by Babcock Galleries

George Washington Crossing the Delaware, 1968
SANTE GRAZIANI (born 1920)
Acrylic on canvas, 36 x 45¼, 91 x 115
Lent by Seyfarth, Shaw, Fairweather & Geraldson

Red, White and Blue Rainbow, 1970
SANTE GRAZIANI
Acrylic on canvas, 40 x 40, 111 x 111
Lent by Babcock Galleries

The Prisoner's Flag, 1966
MARIE-LOUISE D'OTRANGE MASTAI (born 1920)
Oil on acetate, 8½ x 13½, 21.5 x 34
Lent by Mr. and Mrs. Boleslaw Mastai

Mobility '76 and New Glory, 1968
LEONARD LORCH (born 1947)
Oil on anodized aluminum, 72 x 72, 182 x 182
Lent by the Artist

Washington Crossing the Delaware, 1970
J. P. EVANS (born 1947)
Acrylic on canvas, 32 x 48, 81 x 122
Lent by The Touchstone Gallery

Stripes and Stars, 1969
JOHN CASTAGNO (born 1930)
Acrylic on canvas, 30 x 40, 76 x 102
Lent by the Artist

Flag Factory, 1970
CHARLES BRAGG (born 1931)
Oil on board, 10 x 11¾, 26 x 30
Lent by Mr. and Mrs. Alvin Wolf

Flamingo Capsule, 1970
JAMES ROSENQUIST (born 1933)
Oil on canvas, four panels, 114 x 276, 290 x 700
Lent by Leo Castelli Gallery

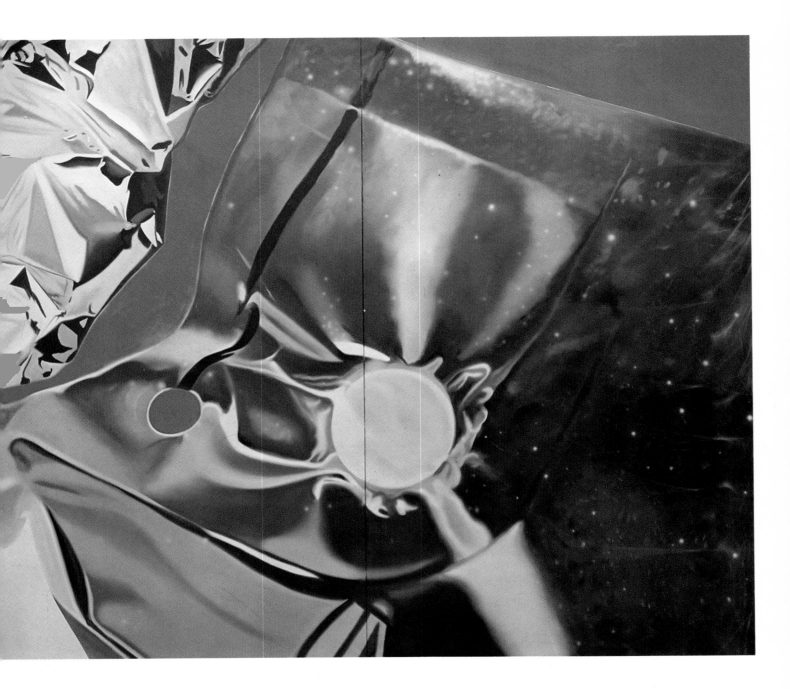

The Spirit of '76, 1974
FRED OTNES (born 1925)
Mixed media, 25 x 20, 64 x 51
Lent by Newspaper Advertising Bureau

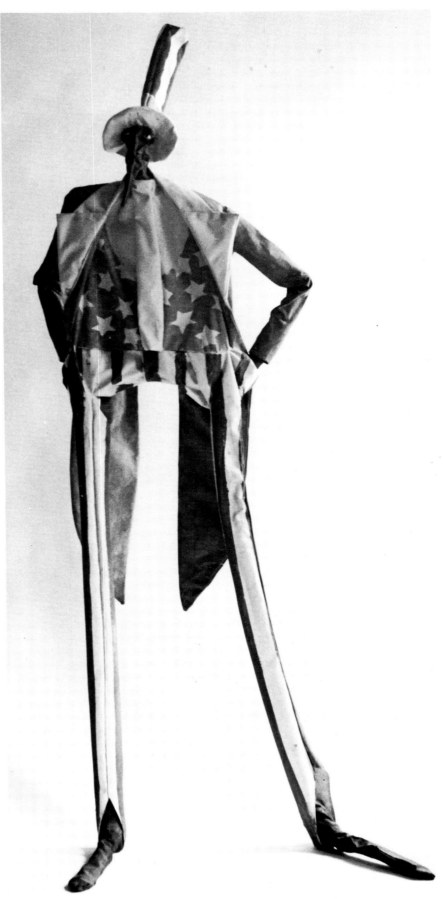

Uncle Sam, 1971
WILLIAM KING (born 1925)
Painted canvas and wood, 82 x 28, 208 x 71
Lent by Terry Dintenfass, Inc.

Iwo Jima, c. 1970
GEORGE FOURNIER (born 1890)
Oil on galvanized iron, 14 x 27½, 36 x 70
Lent by N. F. Karlins

Goodbye America, 1970
CHARLES S. KLABUNDE (born 1935)
Colored etching, 23¾ x 7⅞, 60 x 20
Lent by Prints Division, The New York Public Library,
Astor, Lenox and Tilden Foundations

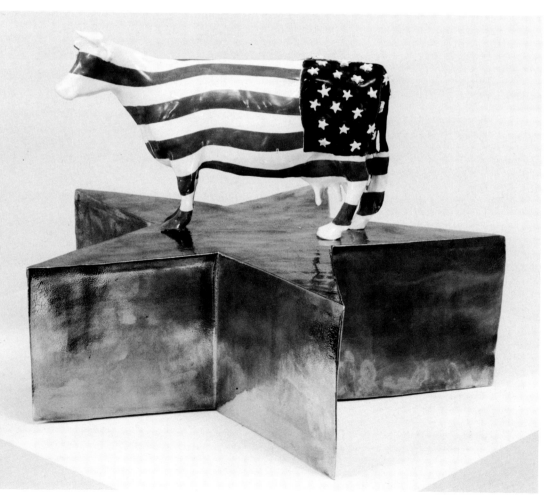

Red, White and Blue Cow, 1970
BILL LOMBARDO (born 1945)
Ceramic, 15 x 20, 38 x 50
Lent by Helen B. Stern

Super Patriot, 1972
NICK ABDALLA (born 1939)
Lithograph, 24½ x 20, 63 x 51
Lent by the Artist

Washington Crossing the Delaware, 1972
CHARLES SANTORE (born 1935)
Acrylic on canvas, 12 x 12, 30 x 30
Lent by Olenka and Charles Santore

Jewish Brides on American Rooftops, 1973
LEAH FRIEDMAN (born 1931)
Acrylic on canvas, 36 x 108, 91 x 274
Lent by Mr. and Mrs. Norman Hirschl

American Indian #4, 1972
FRITZ SCHOLDER (born 1937)
Lithograph, 30 x 22, 76 x 56
Lent by the Artist

Watergate, 1973
HENRY HARRIS (born 1934)
Acrylic on canvas, 40 x 36, 101 x 91
Lent by the Artist

Sleeping Star Lady, 1973
ROBERT BRUCE MUIRHEAD (born 1939)
Oil on canvas, 28 x 32, 72 x 82
Lent by FAR Gallery

Gun Carriage, 1973
FRANK LITTO (born 1919)
Painted wood inlay, 73 x 122 x 2, 185 x 309 x 5
Lent by Louis K. Meisel Gallery

The Patriot, 1973
PAUL ROADARMEL (born 1942)
Acrylic polymer, 24 x 16, 61 x 41
Lent Anonymously

Patrol From Yuma, 1974
WILLIAM SCHENCK (born 1947)
Acrylic on canvas, 65¼ x 73¼, 165 x 186
Lent by Louis K. Meisel Gallery

The New Spirit of '76, 1974
CAROL WALD (born 1935)
Model collage, 11½ x 8½, 29 x 21.5
Lent by City of Cleveland

Theme Was America, 1974
KATHERINE CROWLEY TRAVIS (born 1897)
Acrylic on canvas, 24 x 18, 61 x 46
Lent by the Artist

City Hall Flag, N.Y., 1975
BARCLAY FERGUSON (born 1924)
Acrylic on canvas, 40 x 50, 101 x 126.5
Lent by Lieutenant Commander J. D. Cicio, U.S.N.

USA, 1975
ILSE GETZ (born 1917)
Collage, 10 x 8, 25 x 20
Lent by the Artist

Big Three, 1975
MAY STEVENS (born 1924)
Acrylic on canvas, 72 x 90, 182.5 x 228
Allentown Art Museum Collection,
Gift of The American Academy of Arts and Letters, Hassam Fund, 1976

Eagle With 13 Stars, 1975
ALICE W. NICHOLS (born 1906)
Graphite rubbing and crayon, 22 x 30, 56 x 76
Lent by the Artist

Making the Flag (No. 2) Betsy Ross, 1976, 1975
ERNIE HENFELD (born 1927)
Oil on board, 42 x 34, 107 x 86
Lent by Kennedy Galleries, Inc.

From An American Album, 1975
CAROL WALD
Oil on canvas, 16 x 20, 41 x 51
Lent by Gail Ebach Ross

The American Flag, 1975
J. MAURER (born 1951)
Serigraph on Plexiglas with 117 one dollar bills, 30 x 55½, 76 x 140.5
Allentown Art Museum Collection, 1975

Two Centuries of the Stars and Stripes, 1976
MARIE-LOUISE D'OTRANGE MASTAI
Oil on acetate, 36 x 36, 91 x 91
Lent by Mr. and Mrs. Boleslaw Mastai

The Flag As Popular Postcard Art, c. 1880-1940
(Eighty slides of these will be projected continuously
during the run of the exhibition.)
ANONYMOUS
35 mm. transparencies, photographed by John Kosmer
Lent by Carol Wald

ARTISTS IN THE EXHIBITION

Photograph credits: John Kress Bachman, 7, 78. Geoffrey Clements, 85. George M. Cushing, 47. Christopher Danes, 84. Pedro E. Guerrero, 36. Helga Photo Studio, Inc., 23, 50. Ted Hill Photograph, 78. Honolulu Academy of Arts, 37. The Jones-Gessling Studio, 82. William Lukes, 40, 65. Edward Meneely, 59. Walter Rosenblum, 64. Studio Nine, Inc., 80. Wadsworth Atheneum, Hartford, 35.

LENDERS TO THE EXHIBITION

Abby Aldrich Rockefeller Folk Art Collection,
   Williamsburg, Virginia
Nick Abdalla, Albuquerque, New Mexico
The American Academy of Arts and Letters, New York
Babcock Galleries, New York
The Barenholtz Collection, Princeton, New Jersey
Berry-Hill Galleries, New York
The Trustees of the Boston Public Library, Massachusetts
John Castagno, Philadelphia
Leo Castelli Gallery, New York
Lieutenant Commander J. D. Cicio, U.S.N.,
   Arlington, Virginia
City of Cleveland, Ohio
The Columbus Gallery of Fine Arts, Ohio
Dallas Museum of Fine Arts, Texas
Daughters of Hawaii
   at Queen Emma Summer Palace, Honolulu
H. Richard Dietrich, Jr., Philadelphia
Terry Dintenfass, Inc., New York
The Dinwiddie Mantle and Victorius Collection,
   Warm Springs, Virginia
Stevan Dohanos, Westport, Connecticut
FAR Gallery, New York
Ilse Getz, Newtown, Connecticut
Greenville County Museum of Art, South Carolina
Henry Harris, Philadelphia
Hirschl & Adler Galleries, New York
Mr. and Mrs. Norman Hirschl, New York
The Historical Society of Pennsylvania, Philadelphia
Mr. and Mrs. G. William Holland, Gladwyne, Pennsylvania
Indiana University Art Museum, Bloomington
Indianapolis Museum of Art, Indiana
Jasper Johns, New York
N. F. Karlins, New York
Annie S. Kemerer Museum, Bethlehem, Pennsylvania
Kennedy Galleries, Inc., New York
M. Knoedler & Company, Inc., New York
Kronen Gallery, New York
Mr. and Mrs. Joe M. Leonard, Jr., Gainesville, Texas
The Library of Congress, Washington, D.C.
Leonard Lorch, Woodmere, Long Island, New York

The Los Angeles Athletic Club, California
The Mariners Museum, Newport News, Virginia
Mr. and Mrs. Boleslaw Mastai, New York
Louis K. Meisel Gallery, New York
Cyril Miles, Detroit, Michigan
Museum of African Art, Washington, D.C.
Museum of the American Indian, New York
Museum of Art, Carnegie Institute, Pittsburgh
Museum of the City of New York
Museum of Fine Arts, Springfield, Massachusetts
The Museum of Modern Art, New York
National Gallery of Art, Washington, D.C.
Mr. and Mrs. Walter A. Netsch, Chicago, Illinois
The New York Historical Society
The New York Public Library
The Newark Museum, New Jersey
Newspaper Advertising Bureau, New York
Alice W. Nichols, Muncie, Indiana
Peabody Museum, Salem, Massachusetts
Philadelphia Museum of Art, Pennsylvania
Pioneer Museum and Haggin Galleries, Stockton, California
Mr. and Mrs. Leo Rabkin, New York
Gail Ebach Ross, Columbiaville, Michigan
Olenka and Charles Santore, Philadelphia
Fritz Scholder, Scottsdale, Arizona
Seyfarth, Shaw, Fairweather & Geraldson, Washington, D.C.
Mr. and Mrs. Victor D. Spark, New York
Springfield Art Museum, Missouri
Helen B. Stern, Washington, D.C.
Warren Sturgis, New York
The Touchstone Gallery, Inc., New York
Katherine Crowley Travis, Grosse Pointe, Michigan
University of Nebraska Art Galleries, Lincoln
Robert C. Vose, Jr., Boston
Wadsworth Atheneum, Hartford, Connecticut
Carol Wald, New York
Walker Art Center, Minneapolis, Minnesota
Whitney Museum of American Art, New York
Edna B. Wilmot, Elkhart, Indiana
Mr. and Mrs. Alvin Wolf, Miami, Florida